FIND OUT ABOUT
FLIGHT

**With 18 projects
and more than
240 pictures**

PETER MELLETT

ARMADILLO

This edition is published by Armadillo,
an imprint of Anness Publishing Ltd, Blaby Road, Wigston,
Leicestershire LE18 4SE; info@anness.com

www.annesspublishing.com

If you like the images in this book and would like to
investigate using them for publishing, promotions or
advertising, please visit our website www.practicalpictures.com
for more information.

Publisher: Joanna Lorenz
Managing Editor, Children's Books: Sue Grabham
Editors: Charlotte Evans and Lucy Doncaster
Consultant: Chris Oxlade
Photographer: John Freeman
Stylists: Marion Elliot and Melanie Williams
Designer: Caroline Grimshaw
Picture Researcher: Liz Eddison
Illustrator: Dave Bowyer
Production Controller: Ben Worley

The publishers would also like to thank the following children, and their parents, for
appearing in this book: Emily Askew, Sara Barnes, Maria Bloodworth, David Callega,
Aaron Dumetz, Laurence de Freitas, Alistair Fulton, Anton Goldbourne, Sasha Howarth,
Jon Leming, Jessica Moxley, Ifunanya Obi, Emily Preddie, Elen Rhys, Nicola Twiner
and Joe Westbrook.

A CIP catalogue record for this book is available from the British Library.

PUBLISHER'S NOTE
Although the advice and information in this book are believed to be accurate and true at
the time of going to press, neither the authors nor the publisher can accept any legal
responsibility or liability for any errors or omissions that may have been made nor for any
inaccuracies nor for any loss, harm or injury that comes about from following instructions
or advice in this book.

Manufacturer: Anness Publishing Ltd, Blaby Road, Wigston,
Leicestershire LE18 4SE, England
For Product Tracking go to: www.annesspublishing.com/tracking
Batch: 0359-21017-1127

PICTURE CREDITS (b=bottom, t=top, m=middle, l=left, r=right)
Air France: page 11ml. Heather Angel: page 30b. Austin J. Brown: pages 51bl, 52t. Bruce Coleman Ltd: page 33; /Jane Burton: page 30t; /John Cancalosi: page 32; /Michael Kline: page 19bl; /Gordon Langsbury: page 25b; /Hans Reinhard: page 11t; /Kim Taylor: pages 24b, 25t, 31tr. Liz Eddison: page 45tr; /Royal Aeronautical Society: page 48br. Mary Evans Picture Library: page 60t, m. GreyTrafalgar: page 63l. Mansell Collection: pages 60b, 61tl. Dragos Muresan: page 63tr. Nature Photographers Ltd/Roger Tidman: page 7t. Papillo Photographic: pages 4tr, 28bl, bm, br, 29tl. Popperfoto: page 53b. Quadrant: pages 5t, 7br, 14tl, 34br, 35bl, br, 37tr, 41m, b, 45bl, 49tl, b, 50t, 51t, br, 52br, 53m, 62t; /Paul Bowen Photography: page 45tl; /Flight International: page 21br; /Flight/Wagner: page 37tl; /Peter R. Foster: page 49tr; /Erik Simonsen: pages 11mr, 53t. Reaction Engines Ltd: page 63br. Rolls-Royce plc: page 44br. Spacecharts: pages 4br, 56t, 57tl, m, br, 58t, 62b; /NASA: pages 56b, 57tr. Trip: page 52bl; /T. Legate: page 12br; /T. Malcolm: page 34t; /R. Marsh: page 15bl; /Picturesque/Bill Terry: page 11b; /P. Ridley: page 17t; /J. Ringland: page 22br; /C. Smedley: page 40bl; /Streano/Havens: page 41t; /TH-Foto Werbung: page 16t; /Derek Thomas: page 21bl. Zefa Pictures: pages 5bl, 7bl, 10tr, 15tl, tr, br, 17br, 21tr, 28tl, 29tl, 31tl, b, 36, 40br, 44t, 45br, 48bl, 54t, 55bl, 61b; /J.Sedlmeier: page 61tr.

CONTENTS

WHAT IS FLIGHT?

Think of flight and you think of things like birds and insects, paper darts and planes, bullets and footballs. All of these can move swiftly through the air, but are they all really flying? To answer this question, imagine you are launching a paper dart into the air. It glides away from you and finally lands back on the ground. Now throw a ball in exactly the same way. It hits the ground much sooner than the paper dart. We say that the paper dart was flying, but the ball was not. This is because bullets, footballs, stones and arrows are all projectiles. They do not really fly because they have nothing to keep them up in the air. Birds, aircraft, rockets and balloons do fly – they stay off the ground longer than something that is simply thrown.

Animal power
Birds, insects and bats all have wings. They use their wings to hold themselves up in the air and move along. Muscles provide power for take-off.

Balloons
This balloon is filled with a gas called helium. It is lighter than air so the balloon floats upwards, just like a cork floats upwards in water. This is how hot-air balloons and airships are able to fly. Before aircraft were invented, the only way people could make a sustained flight was by a lighter-than-air craft, such as a balloon or an airship.

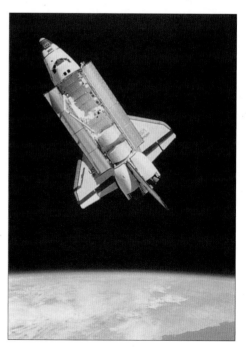

Spaceflight
The Space Shuttle was launched into Space by powerful booster rockets. It used its own rocket engines to reach an orbit 300km/ 180 miles above the Earth. Earth's force of gravity would act like a tether, keeping the Shuttle in orbit, while the Shuttle's speed prevented it from falling back to the ground.

Planes
Aeroplanes (or airplanes) have wings like birds to hold them up in the air, but they also have engines. Engine power is needed to push them through the air and provide enough power to help them take off from the ground.

Tether

Flying a kite
A kite is lifted into the air by a blowing wind. A long string, called a tether, holds the kite at an angle to the wind. The rushing air pushes against the kite, pushing it upwards and keeping it in the air. If the wind drops or the tether breaks, the kite will fall back to the ground.

Gliders
These aircraft have no engines, so they have to be towed into the air by small powered planes or by machines on the ground. On release, their wings hold them up in the air as they glide slowly back to the ground in a gentle spiral. The pilot controls the glider's flight by searching for rising air currents and by altering the shape of the glider's wings.

WINGS AND LIFT

FLAP your arms up and down like a bird – you cannot take off because you are not designed to fly. You are the wrong shape and your muscles are not strong enough. Birds have wings and powerful muscles that enable them to fly. Flapping provides a force called thrust, which moves a bird forwards through the air. A bird's wings are a special shape, called an aerofoil (airfoil). In an aerofoil, the top side is more curved than the underneath. This shape helps to keep a bird up in the air, even when its wings are not flapping. When an aerofoil wing moves through the air, it creates an upwards push. This push is a force called lift. It works in the opposite direction to the weight of the object (due to the force of gravity), which pulls an object down towards the ground. There are many different shapes and sizes of birds, gliders and planes, but they all have aerofoil wings.

If you blow across a sheet of paper it reduces the pressure of the air above the paper. The stronger pressure beneath lifts the paper up.

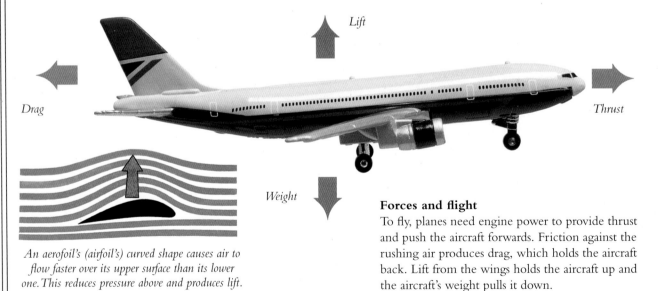

Lift

Drag

Thrust

Weight

An aerofoil's (airfoil's) curved shape causes air to flow faster over its upper surface than its lower one. This reduces pressure above and produces lift.

Forces and flight
To fly, planes need engine power to provide thrust and push the aircraft forwards. Friction against the rushing air produces drag, which holds the aircraft back. Lift from the wings holds the aircraft up and the aircraft's weight pulls it down.

Wings and soaring

This bird is soaring through the air without flapping its wings. As its wings slice through the air, the force of lift pushes up on them. The faster the bird's speed, the greater the lift. It is able to glide like this for many hours.

Helicopters

Planes have fixed wings. They must rush through the air so that their wings work. Helicopters have long thin aerofoil wings called rotor blades. Powerful engines whirl the blades around so that the blades produce lift. Helicopters can hover, or fly forwards, backwards and sideways, as well as straight up and down.

Taking off

Most planes need long runways to take off. They speed along, getting faster and faster, until the lift pushing up is greater than the weight pulling down, allowing them to leave the ground.

MAKE A FLYING MODEL

BIRDS, gliders and planes all have wings. Their wings can be all sorts of different shapes and sizes, but they all have the same aerofoil (airfoil) design. This means that the top side of the wing is more curved than the underneath. From a tiny sparrow to a huge airliner, the aerofoil shape provides lift when air moves over it. Air flows faster over the curved upper surface than the flatter, lower surface. This reduces the air pressure above the wing and allows the stronger air pressure underneath to lift it up.

You can make and test a model aerofoil by following the instructions in these projects. They will show you how moving air lifts wings upwards. In the first project, a frisbee is a circular aerofoil shaped like a dish. Just like a straight wing, air flows faster over its top surface than its underneath. The frisbee spins as it flies. This motion helps to steady it.

You will need:
a large plate, cardboard, pencil,
scissors, ruler, adhesive tape.

Make a frisbee

1 Place the plate face down on the cardboard and draw around it with a pencil. Cut out the circle. Draw slots 2cm/1in deep around the edge and cut along these as well.

2 The cut slots around the edge will make tabs. Bend the tabs down slightly. Overlap them a little and stick them together with small pieces of adhesive tape.

3 Fly your frisbee outside, away from people. Hold it at the front and spin it away from you and up.

Make an aerofoil (airfoil)

1 Cut out a rectangle of paper about 15cm/6in wide and 20cm/8in long. Draw in the middle line.

2 Fold the paper over. Use tape to stick the top edge about 1cm/½in away from the bottom edge.

3 Cut out and stick on a small fin near the rear edge of your wing. This will keep the wing facing into the airflow when you test it.

M A T E R I A L S

You will need: paper, pencil, ruler, scissors, adhesive tape, glue, plastic drinking straw, thick cotton yarn.

4 With a sharp pencil, poke a hole through the top and bottom of your wing, near the front edge. Push a straw through the holes and glue it in place in the middle.

5 Cut a 1m/3ft long piece of thick cotton yarn and thread it through the straw. Make sure the cotton can slide easily through the straw and does not catch.

Hold the cotton tight and blow air from a fan or hair dryer over the wing. Watch it take off! Do you know how this happens?

AIR RESISTANCE

WHEN you are swimming, you have to push your way through the water. All the time, the water is resisting you and slowing you down. In the same way, things that fly have to push their way through the air. Air clings to their surfaces as they rush through it. The result is a backwards pull called drag, or air resistance, which works against the direction of flight. Drag is the force that slows down anything that is flying through the air. Drag depends on shape. Fat, lumpy shapes with sharp edges create a lot of drag. They disturb the air and make it swirl about as they move along. Sleek, streamlined shapes have low drag and can fly the fastest. They hardly disturb the air as they cut smoothly through it. For any shape, increasing the speed increases the drag. Double the speed creates four times the amount of drag. The result is that drag limits how fast anything can fly.

Parachutes fall slowly because they trap air underneath. They are designed to have very high drag.

When an aircraft is in flight, the angle its wings make to the airflow is called the angle of attack. If the angle of attack is increased, the amount of lift also increases.

If the angle of attack becomes too great, lift drops suddenly. The smooth flow of air over the wing is broken, creating turbulence, increasing drag and reducing lift.

Angle of attack

Turbulence

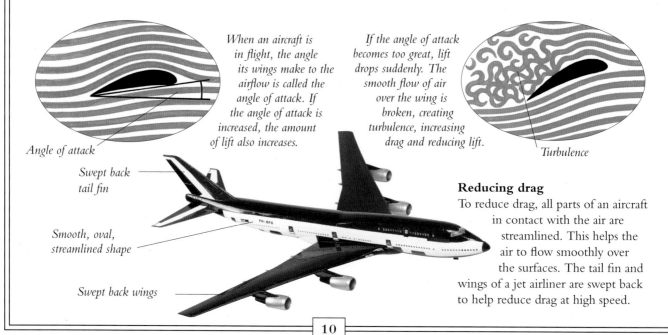

Swept back tail fin

Smooth, oval, streamlined shape

Swept back wings

Reducing drag

To reduce drag, all parts of an aircraft in contact with the air are streamlined. This helps the air to flow smoothly over the surfaces. The tail fin and wings of a jet airliner are swept back to help reduce drag at high speed.

Birds must slow down before they land. This owl has tipped up its wings so that the undersides face forwards. It has also lowered and spread out its tail feathers to act as a brake. Drag increases suddenly, lift decreases and the bird drops to its landing place.

The Lockheed SR-71 lands at over 350km per hour/ 210 miles per hour. A parachute helps it slow down, as ordinary brakes on its wheels would take too long.

Concorde could fly at a speed of over 2,000km per hour/1,200 miles per hour. Its wings were swept back to reduce drag to a minimum. If its wings stuck straight out they would have been ripped off at this speed.

Coming in to land, an airliner uses flaps on its wings to increase lift at low speeds. During flight, these flaps are retracted to reduce drag.

STREAMLINING AND SHAPE

Tʜɪɴᴋ of a sleek canoe moving through water. Its streamlined shape makes hardly any ripples as it passes by. Streamlined shapes also move easily through air. We say that they have low drag. Drag is also called air resistance. It is the force that works against the direction of flight. Drag is affected by shape. Angular shapes have more drag than rounded ones. Design and test your own streamlined shapes, or make a model parachute and find out how its shape is designed to have high drag to make it fall slowly.

Air flows in gentle curves around the streamlined shape (top). Angles or sharp curves break up the flow and increase drag.

Shape race
Make different shapes (*as shown on the right*) from balls of modelling clay all the same size. Race your shapes in water – the most streamlined shape should reach the bottom first.

Star shape

Square shape

Teardrop shape

How much of a splash would you make diving into a pool? This diver's streamlined shape will help her cut cleanly through the water to dive deep down.

12

Make a parachute

You will need:
thin fabric, a large plate,
felt-tipped pen, scissors, needle,
cotton thread, adhesive tape,
plastic cotton reel.

1 Use the felt-tipped pen to draw around the plate on the fabric. Carefully cut out the circle to make the parachute's canopy.

2 Make about eight equally spaced marks around the edge of the circle. Use a needle to sew on a 30cm/12in long piece of thread at each point you have marked.

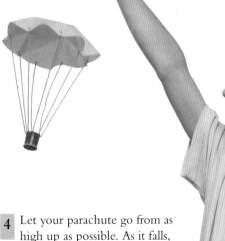

3 Use adhesive tape to tape the free end of each thread to the cotton reel. Be sure to use a plastic reel, as a wooden one will be too heavy for your parachute.

4 Let your parachute go from as high up as possible. As it falls, the canopy will open and fill with air. The larger the canopy, the slower the parachute will fall.

GLIDING AND SOARING

A glider is towed into the air attached to a cable. Its long, thin wings give maximum lift and minimum drag for their size. If a glider flies level in still air, drag forces slow it down and the wings lose their lift. So, to keep up speed, a glider flies on a gradual downwards slope.

Watch a small bird as it flies. It flaps its wings very fast for almost the whole time. Large birds, however, often glide with their wings stretched out flat and still. They can do this because their wings create enough lift to keep them up in the air without flapping flight. Soaring birds, such as albatrosses and condors, fly for hours hardly moving their wings at all. They gain height by using rising air currents over the land and sea.

Gliders are aircraft that do not have engines. They have wings like those of soaring birds. They are pulled along by small aircraft or by winches on the ground, until the lift generated by their wings keeps them airborne. Glider pilots seek out rising air currents, called thermals, to lift their aircraft up.

Going up

Pilots look for thermals (rising air currents) to gain height. Thermals happen where the wind is forced upwards by cliffs or hillsides, or where the air is heated by the ground. Hot air rises because it is pushed up by the cold air around it. The glider circles inside the thermal, steadily gaining height as the rising air carries it up. At the top of the thermal the effect is weaker, so the pilot stops circling and flies straight on.

Leaving the thermal

Going into the thermal

Rising hot air carries glider up

Paraglider

A paraglider's wing shape is made by air blowing into pockets on its leading edge. The pilot steers from side to side and can ride up thermals.

Albatrosses have long narrow wings. This wing shape helps them to glide for enormous distances on air currents blowing over the open ocean. At more than 3m/9ft long, albatrosses have the longest wingspan of any bird.

This picture shows the inside of a glider's cockpit, high above ground. The left-hand dial gives forward air speed. The middle dial shows the rate of climb or descent (how fast the glider is going up or down). The last dial on the right shows the glider's altitude, or height above ground.

Hang glider

Made from strong, thin material stretched over a framework of aluminium poles, a hang glider is very light. The material on the hang glider's wing is stretched into an aerofoil (airfoil) shape to produce lift. To steer the hang glider, the pilot moves a control bar forwards to climb and backwards to dive.

KITES AND SAILS

Flown from poles during festivals, windsock kites have open 'mouths' to catch the wind. Like all kites, they will only fly when the wind blows against them.

Have you ever been blown over by the wind? Wind is moving air – it pushes against anything standing in its path. You can fly a kite because it is held up in the air by the force of the wind pushing against it. A string, called a tether, joins the kite to the ground and holds it at the correct angle to the wind. You can feel tension in the tether pulling on your hand. The tension is the result of the wind blowing against the kite and lifting it up. If the tether broke, the kite would no longer be held at the correct angle and it would fall to the ground. When there is no wind, a kite can still be made to fly by pulling it through the air.

Lift
Air blowing into the kite creates lift.

Flying a kite
What makes a kite fly? Wind is deflected downwards when it blows against a kite. This pushes the kite upwards and creates lift and drag. The tether keeps the kite at an angle to the wind (the angle of attack). In a good breeze, a kite's weight is very small compared to the forces of lift and drag.

Drag
Air moving over and around the kite causes drag.

Weight
The kite's weight pulls it down towards the Earth.

Pull on tether
The tether holds the kite at an angle to the wind.

Flat kite

The oldest and simplest kite is the plane surface, or flat, kite. It has a simple diamond shape and a flat frame. Kites like these have been flown for thousands of years. Flat kites look very impressive strung together to make a spectacular, writhing pattern in the sky.

Box kite

A square-shaped box kite is more complicated to make than a flat kite, but it is more stable and has better lift. It does not need a tail to keep it upright. Box kites can be a combination of triangles and rectangles. Large box kites have been used to lift people off the ground in the past.

Parasail

A parasail is a kite that can lift a person into the air. It does not rely on the wind, but instead it is towed behind a boat or a car. A parasail looks like a parachute that has been divided into different parts, called cells. Each cell can work independently from the others, catching as much wind as possible and providing more upthrust. Parasails usually fly about 50m/150ft above the ground.

MAKE A KITE

F OR 3,000 years people have been making and flying kites. The first kites were made from cloth or paper attached to a light bamboo frame. As time went by, the simple secret of building a good kite was discovered – make it as light as possible for its size. Some kites can fly in very gentle breezes. Their surfaces are wide so that the breeze has a large area to push against. Their low weight means that a small amount of lift is enough to make them take off into the sky. The kite design shown in this project has been used for many hundreds of years. Try flying it in a steady wind. You might have to experiment with the position of the bridle and the length of the tail.

You will need: two plant canes (one about twice as long as the other), ruler, pen, string, scissors, adhesive tape, sheet of thin fabric or plastic, fabric glue, paper.

This kite's long tail will help to keep it upright and stop it from spinning around.

Make a kite

1 To make the frame, mark the middle of the short cane and mark one-third of the way up the long cane. Tie the canes together at the marks with string.

2 Tape string around the ends of the canes and secure it at the top. This will stop the canes from moving and it will also support the edges of your kite.

3 Lay the frame on top of the sheet of material or plastic. Cut all around it, about 3cm/1⅛in away from the edge. This will give you enough to fold over the string outline.

4 Fold each edge of the material over the frame and stick the edges down firmly with fabric glue (or adhesive tape if you are making the kite from plastic). Leave the glue to dry.

5 Tie a piece of string to the long cane, as shown – this is called the bridle. Tie the end of the ball of string to the middle of the bridle to make the tether.

6 To make the tail, fold sheets of paper in zigzags. Tie them at about 25cm/10in intervals along a piece of string that is about twice as long as the kite. Glue or tie the tail to the bottom tip of the kite.

This kite has been made to look like a face with a long trailing moustache. Highly decorative designs can make the simplest kite look very effective. Have fun experimenting with the basic kite design shown in this project.

7 Now your kite is ready to fly! With the wind blowing on your back, reel out about 10m/30ft of tether. Ask an adult to gently launch the kite into the air. If it is not very windy, run forwards into the breeze, pulling the kite to get it airborne. Now you have built this kite, try experimenting with other materials and shapes to find which is best.

LIGHTER THAN AIR

OIL floats on water because it is lighter than water. We say that oil is less dense than water. This means that a bottle full of oil weighs less than the same bottle full of water. Water pushes upwards on the oil with a force called upthrust. Watch smoke rising from a fire. Hot air is less dense than the cold air around it. The hot air floats upwards, taking the smoke with it. A hot-air balloon is simply a huge bag full of hot air. It experiences upthrust from the cold air around it. The balloon takes off because the upthrust is greater than its own weight pulling it down. Like balloons, airships are lighter than the air around them. Modern airships are filled with a gas called helium, which is seven times lighter than air. Hot-air balloons and airships fly because the air around them pushes them upwards, just like oil floating on water.

A candle heats the air around it. Snuff out the flame and the smoke is carried upwards by the rising hot air.

Oil and water
Oil floats on water because it is less dense than water. The water surrounding the oil pushes upwards on it. This push is called upthrust.

FACT BOX
• The first ever balloon passengers were a sheep, a duck and a cockerel. They were sent up to make sure it was safe for people to travel by this new form of transport.

• The first balloon flight took place over Paris on November 21, 1783. It lasted 25 minutes.

• The first airship flight took place in France in 1852. Henri Giffard steered a steam-driven craft for 28km/18 miles at an average speed of 8km per hour/5 miles per hour.

• At 244m/750ft long, the world's largest airship was the German *Hindenburg*. In 1937 it was destroyed when it burst into flames on landing, killing 35 people.

The first aviators

In 1783, brothers Joseph and Jacques Montgolfier built an enormous paper balloon and lit a fire underneath it. The balloon sailed into the sky, safely carrying two people into the air for the very first journey by hot-air balloon.

Hot-air balloons

Modern hot-air balloons are twice as tall as a house. They are made of nylon and can carry about five people in a basket hanging underneath. All hot-air balloons can only go where the wind blows them.

Modern airship

This airship uses helium to float. Unlike a hot-air balloon it has engines and propellers to drive it along. The pilot steers by moving fins on the tail.

Airships in the 1930s were huge. They were filled with hydrogen gas that easily burst into flames, making the airships very dangerous.

MAKE A HOT–AIR BALLOON

Hot-air balloons rise into the sky because the hot air inside them is lighter than the cold air outside. The main part of the balloon is called the envelope. Hot air rises into the envelope from gas burners. The envelope fills with about 2.5 tons of hot air (the same as the weight of two cars). This amount of hot air pushes cold air around the balloon out of the way. The weight of the cold air is about 3.5 tons. The result is about 1 ton of upthrust, enough to lift the balloon, its passengers and bottles of gas off the ground. You can make and fly a model hot-air balloon to see it rise in exactly the same way.

You will need:
pencil, cardboard, ruler, scissors, sheets
of tissue paper, glue stick, hair dryer.

Stabilize a balloon
Try adding modelling clay to the string of a helium balloon until the balloon hangs steady. The force downwards (weight) now equals the force upwards (upthrust).

Gas burners
Roaring gas burners heat the air inside the balloon. It takes more than half an hour to fill the balloon's envelope. When the envelope is full, the balloon is launched by untying ropes that hold it to the ground.

Make a hot-air balloon

1 Draw a petal-shaped template on card and cut it out. The shape should be 30cm/12in long and 12cm/5in across with a flat bottom edge.

2 Draw around your template on to seven pieces of tissue paper. Be careful not to rip the paper with the tip of your pencil.

3 Carefully cut out the shapes you have drawn. You should now have seven petals that are all the same size and shape.

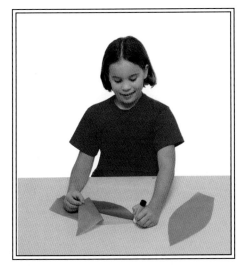

4 Glue along one edge of a petal. Lay another petal on top and press down. Open out and stick on another petal in the same way. Keep going until the balloon is complete.

5 To make your balloon fly, hold its neck open and fill the inside with hot air from a hair dryer. After ten seconds, switch off the hair dryer and let go of your balloon to launch it into the air.

BIRDS IN FLIGHT

MUSCLE-POWERED flight is very hard work. Although we have tried, no human has ever flown by flapping artificial wings. Compared to us, birds are light and very powerful. They are perfectly designed to stay up in the air. Birds' wings are covered in feathers – one of the strongest and lightest natural materials known. Their wings have an aerofoil (airfoil) shape to provide lift, while their tail feathers help with steering and braking. Birds flap their wings hard to take off and climb into the air. A bird needs enormous flight muscles to provide enough power for flight – they can account for up to half the weight of a bird. These muscles are supplied by blood that is pumped by a large heart beating very fast. For humans to fly, we would need a chest the size of a barrel, arms 3m/9ft long, legs like broom handles and a head the size of an apple – as well as thousands of feathers!

Barb

Every feather has a hollow tube running down its centre. Microscopic hooks lock each barb together so that air cannot pass through the feather.

Primary feathers

Flying feathers
The large primary flight feathers on the end of each wing produce most of the power for flight. These feathers can also be closed together or spread apart to control flight. Smaller secondary flight feathers on the inner wing form the curve that provides lift. The innermost feathers shape the wing into the bird's body and help to prevent turbulence in flight.

Secondary feathers

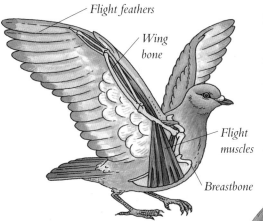

Flight feathers

Wing bone

Flight muscles

Breastbone

A bird's body

Flight feathers are connected to thin bones at the end of each wing. Bird bones are light – most are hollow and filled with air. The large flight muscles are anchored to the breastbone at the front of a bird's chest.

FACT BOX

• A sparrow's heart beats 800 times a minute – when working very hard yours beats at about 120 times a minute.

• Birds are the only animals covered in feathers. A large bird, such as a swan, has about 25,000 feathers, while a tiny hummingbird has only 1,000.

• Arctic terns migrate each year from the Arctic to the Antarctic and back again – a round trip of about 40,000km/6,000 miles.

• The world's largest bird, the ostrich, is simply too heavy to fly. The world's largest flying bird is the Kori bustard, which weighs no more than 18kg/40lb.

On the wing

This owl shows how a bird flies through the air. A bird's wings bend in the middle as they rise upwards. The feathers open to help the air pass through the wings. On the powerful downstroke, the primary flight feathers slice through the air, pushing the air down and back and pulling the bird upwards and forwards.

Peregrine falcons are the fastest animals in the world. Folding back their wings to reduce drag, they dive at their prey at speeds up to 350 km per hour/ 210 miles per hour. The force of the impact breaks the victim's neck.

HOW BIRDS FLY

Look at a large bird, such as a goose, flying in the sky. Can you describe how its wings are moving? Flying birds do not simply flap their wings up and down. Their wings are not stiff and flat – instead, each wing has a joint like an elbow in the middle. This joint allows the wing to bend on the upstroke and flatten on the downstroke. Birds also open and close their flight feathers. On the upstroke, the feathers are separated so that air can pass easily through the wings. On the downstroke, the feathers are held together so that they provide the maximum amount of lift.

Start the project on these pages with a simple water test to feel how a bird's primary flight feathers work. You can then go on to build a model bird to see how birds move their wings in flight.

When a bird raises its wings (the upstroke), its feathers open to allow the air through. Feel the effect by moving your hand through water with your fingers spread open.

During the downstroke, a bird closes its flight feathers so its wings push hard against the air. This pushes the bird up and forwards. Now close your fingers and move your hand through the water. Can you feel a difference?

Make a model bird

1 Start by making the bird's legs. Fold a piece of paper in half lengthways several times until it is about 2.5cm/1in across.

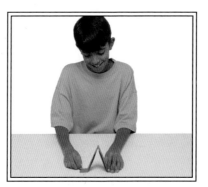

2 Fold the strip in half and make a fold at each end to make the feet. Tape the feet to your work surface to keep your model stable.

3 To make the body, roll a piece of paper into a tube and secure the edge with adhesive tape. Use more tape to stick the body to the legs.

4 To make the wings, fold a piece of paper twice lengthways so that it is about six times longer than it is wide. Fold it into a W shape.

5 Stick the wings on to the body. You have now made a model bird. To mimic how a bird flies, hold one wing tip in each hand.

6 Move your hands in circles one going clockwise, the other anticlockwise. At take-off, a bird's wings make large, round circles.

┤ M A T E R I A L S ├

You will need: sheets of paper, adhesive tape, scissors, glue stick.

8 During the downstroke, you can see how the wings become flatter. To see how a bird's wings move when the bird is flying level, move your hands far apart in small, flat circles.

7 During the upstroke, notice how the wings bend in the middle. Some birds even bang their wings together at the top of the upstroke.

INSECT WINGS

Like all insects, a dragonfly's wings are thin and light. They are strengthened by a network of hollow tubes, called veins.

Dragonfly darter

INSECTS' wings and birds' wings work in different ways. Insects' wings are flat and stiff. They do not have an aerofoil (airfoil) shape, but instead churn up the air to make swirling currents that provide lift. Forward movement is due to the wings pushing backwards as they beat downwards. Flying insects can hover and then dart off in any direction, twisting and turning through the air. They can even fly backwards. Insects control their flight by beating their wings in extremely complicated patterns. Unlike most birds, the upstroke is as powerful as the downstroke. Many flying insects, such as bees, wasps and moths, have two pairs of wings, but some, such as flies and mosquitoes, only have one.

One of the most skilled flying insects is the dragonfly. Most insects flap their wings together, but a dragonfly uses its two pairs of wings separately.

As it beats its front wings down, a whirlwind is stirred up. This passes over the back wings, generating lift. An articulated tail helps the dragonfly steer.

With each beat, the wings push air down and back, moving the dragonfly up and forward. Its wings bend as they flap, giving more control in flight.

Butterflies

Butterflies have
two pairs of wings that
are hooked together so they act like one.
Many butterflies have square-shaped wings
that flap quite slowly. Their wings are covered
with powdery scales. The largest butterflies have
wingspans up to 28cm/10in across.

Beetle wings

A beetle's front wings are hard covers that are used to protect
the flying wings underneath. In flight, the wing covers stick
out, helping to steady the beetle's body.

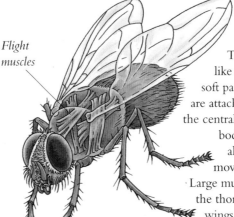

Flight muscles

FACT BOX

• Insects beat their wings at different speeds.
The wings of a large dragonfly beat 35 times
a second and a mosquito 600. The faster the
wings beat, the higher the buzzing sound.

• The record speed for an insect is held by
a dragonfly at 95km per hour/55 miles per
hour. A house fly can reach 6km per hour/
3½ miles per hour.

• There have been dragonflies on Earth for
350 million years.

• Monarch butterflies migrate 400km/1,000
miles across North America each year.

• For its size, a dragonfly generates three
times the lift of the most efficient aircraft.

Insect bodies

The body of this fly is
like a hard box with the
soft parts inside. The wings
are attached to the thorax,
the central part of the insect's
body. Hinged joints
allow each wing to
move in any direction.
Large muscles inside pull on
the thorax, moving the
wings up and down.

AMAZING FLYING ANIMALS

Flying fish swim very fast, close to the surface of the water. With wing-shaped fins stretched out, they leap upwards and forwards into the air, thrashing the water with their tails until they reach take-off.

THE only animals that can fly, apart from birds and insects, are bats. Bats have wings that can push downwards to create lift. Unlike birds, most bats are nocturnal – they sleep in the day and fly at night. A few other sorts of animals can fly through the air, but they cannot control or power their flight with flapping wings. Instead, they glide down through the air in search of food, or to escape from their enemies. These animals include flying frogs, flying squirrels and flying lizards. They jump outwards from high places, moving forwards through the air as they parachute downwards. Flying fish sail along through the air using two fins that look like wings. Their gliding flight only lasts a few seconds, but their speed is much faster than they can swim underwater.

FACT BOX
• Some flying fish can glide along at 50km per hour/30 miles per hour. The record flight for a flying fish lasted 90 seconds and covered more than 1km/½ mile.

• Flying foxes are actually a type of large fruit-eating bat. There are more than 2,000 species, or types, of bat living in the world.

• Flying snakes are able to flatten their bodies to help them glide from tree to tree.

• Some flying frogs jump from a height of 40m/120ft. They glide along, covering about 30m/90ft in only 8 seconds.

• The colugo, or flying lemur, can easily glide 100m/300ft or more between trees.

Flying frog

Flying frogs have enormous webbed feet. They use their feet as parachutes when they jump down from trees in search of insects. Altering the shape of their feet allows them to control their flight. Flying frogs have sticky pads on their toes to help them climb. Using these pads, they can cling to the smoothest leaves and branches in the rainforest.

Flying lizard

A flying lizard has flaps of skin along each side of its body. These are supported by spines hinged to the ribs. When danger threatens, the spines stick out and the lizard glides away.

Flying squirrel

Flying squirrels have folds of thin skin between their front and rear legs. They glide from tree to tree by stretching out their legs to spread the skin wide.

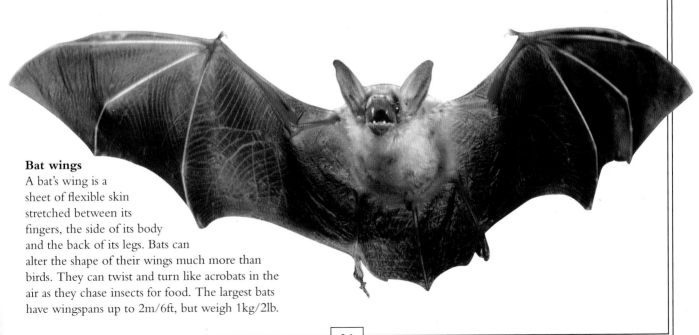

Bat wings

A bat's wing is a sheet of flexible skin stretched between its fingers, the side of its body and the back of its legs. Bats can alter the shape of their wings much more than birds. They can twist and turn like acrobats in the air as they chase insects for food. The largest bats have wingspans up to 2m/6ft, but weigh 1kg/2lb.

PREHISTORIC FLYERS

THE earliest known flying creature is the dragonfly. The first ones lived about 350 million years ago, during a hot swampy time called the Carboniferous Period. Many other flying insects also evolved during the next 150 million years, many of them similar to the insects we know today. About 200 million years ago, the first gliding reptiles appeared. From them evolved giant winged lizards called pterosaurs. The largest pterosaurs had wingspans up to 12m/36ft across. Over 150 million years ago, the first feathered creature, *Archaeopteryx*, lived on Earth. Scientists think it evolved from small dinosaurs and may be the first known bird.

This insect lived about 50 million years ago. It was caught in sticky tree resin. The resin gradually fossilized and changed into amber.

FACT BOX
- Some prehistoric dragonflies had wingspans of up to 1m/3ft across.

- The earliest humans lived less than one million years ago. Modern-looking birds have existed for over 30 million years.

- Modern birds have just two finger bones in each wing. *Archaeopteryx* had all five, complete with claws at the ends.

- Fish fossils are often found near pterosaurs, so these flying lizards may have lived at sea.

- The largest flying animal ever to have existed was a pterosaur called *Quetzalocoatlus*. It had a human-sized body and a wingspan of 12m/36ft – wider than a hang glider.

Gliding reptiles
The first flying reptiles were gliders. *Longisquama* had tall crests along its back that might have opened up like wings and helped it to glide. It probably searched for insects to eat.

Giant pterosaurs

The first true flying reptiles were the pterosaurs. They lived at the same time as the dinosaurs and could reach huge sizes. Their wings were made of skin and their bodies were usually furry. They had light, delicate bones that reduced their weight and helped them fly.

Archaeopteryx

Archaeopteryx had bird-like wings and legs, but a mouth full of teeth and a tail like a lizard. It was thickly feathered, but many scientists do not think it could fly very well. The first fossilized *Archaeopteryx* was found in a quarry in Germany in 1860. Since then six more have been discovered.

Fossilized feathers

This is a fossilized skeleton of an *Archaeopteryx*. When the animal died, all the skin and flesh rotted away. Buried deep underground, the skeleton slowly turned to stone.

AIRCRAFT WINGS

THE smallest microlight carries one person and weighs less than 100kg/200lb. The largest passenger jet carries over 500 people and weighs nearly 400 tons. But whatever the size or shape, all planes have one thing in common – they all have wings. Wings provide the lift aircraft need to hold them up in the air. The shape of the wings depends on how fast and high an aircraft must fly. Swept-back wings are needed for high-speed flight. Broad wings with a large area are needed to carry heavy loads. All wings have moving parts to help the aircraft land, take off and change direction.

This aircraft is called a triplane because it has three sets of wings. Early planes needed more sets of wings to provide enough lift as their speed was slow.

Tail fin

Wing

Tailplane

Fuselage

Propeller

Undercarriage

The parts of an aircraft
This picture shows the names of all the main parts of a small aircraft. They are needed for the aircraft to take off, fly level, change direction and land. The body of the aircraft is called the fuselage and the landing wheels are called the undercarriage. On many aircraft, the undercarriage folds up inside the body of the aircraft during flight to reduce drag. Hinged control surfaces on the tail and the wings are used to steer the aircraft from left to right as well as up and down.

Piper Cadet
Like most planes, this small aircraft is called a monoplane because it has one set of wings. The wings stick straight out from the aircraft's body because it flies fairly slowly. This arrangement provides the greatest lift.

Flaps

Aileron

Flaps

Slats

Spoilers

Flaps and slats

Just before landing, the wings of an airliner become larger to provide more lift at low speed. Parts called slats move out from the front of the wings and flaps stick out from the rear. After landing, spoilers or air brakes are raised to reduce any remaining lift and slow the aircraft down. The aileron is used during flight to change the position of the aircraft. On landing it is kept level to increase the surface area of the wing.

Boeing 747

Wide-bodied jets, like this Boeing 747, fly high and fast. Large wings provide enough lift to carry nearly 400 tons. The wings are tapered and swept back to keep drag low when flying at 1,000km per hour/600 miles per hour. Swept-back wings reduce lift, so a high take-off speed is needed.

Swing-wings

Some military aircraft can move their wings. For high-speed flight, wings are swept backwards in a low-drag triangle shape. To provide lift at lower speeds, the wings are swung forwards, as shown in this picture.

FLYING AN AIRCRAFT

Biplanes have two sets of wings. They are strong, agile and easy to fly and are often used as trainer planes or in acrobatic displays. Biplanes with open cockpits and wings braced with wires and struts were the most common aircraft design until the 1930s.

To make a car turn left or right, all you have to do is turn the steering wheel. To steer a plane, you must move two sets of controls – one with your hands and one with your feet. Moving these controls alters the control surfaces on the plane's wings and tail. Control surfaces are small hinged flaps that affect how air flows around the plane. There are three main types of control surface: the ailerons attached to the rear edge of each wing; the elevators mounted at the rear of the tailplane; and the rudder at the rear of the tail fin. The pilot can also control flight by engine power – more power increases speed and so increases lift. So, an accelerating aircraft flying level will steadily gain height.

Aileron

Aileron

Elevator

Rudder

Aileron

Control surfaces
To turn the aircraft (yaw), the pilot turns the rudder to one side. To make the aircraft descend or climb (pitch), the pilot adjusts the elevators on the tailplane. To roll (tilt or bank) the aircraft to the right or left, the ailerons are raised on one wing and lowered on the other.

Roll
The ailerons on an aircraft operate in opposite directions to each other. When one aileron is raised, the other is lowered. The wing with the lowered aileron rises while the wing with the raised aileron drops.

Pitch
The elevators on the plane's tail are raised or lowered to make the plane's nose rise or fall. Lowering the elevators causes the aircraft's nose to drop, putting the plane into a dive. Raising the elevators causes the aircraft to climb.

Yaw
When the rudder is pushed to one side the aircraft moves left or right. Whichever way the rudder points, the aircraft's nose is deflected in the same direction. The rudder is used together with the ailerons to make a turn.

Turning

When an aircraft
turns, it moves rather
like a cyclist going round a
corner. It banks as it turns, which means that it
leans to one side with one wing higher than the
other. This means that some of the lift from the wings
is used to turn the aircraft and helps it to turn smoothly.

*Inside the cockpit of a modern small aircraft the pilot
moves throttle levers to control engine power. The control
column and pedals move the control surfaces. Dials and
gauges show such things as fuel consumption, flight
direction, altitude and how level the plane is flying.*

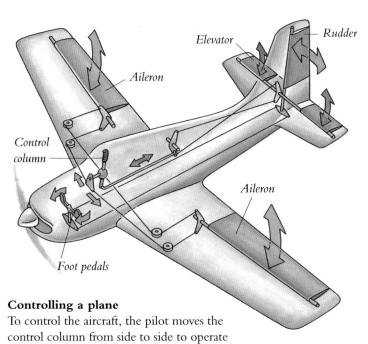

Elevator

Rudder

Aileron

Control
column

Aileron

Foot pedals

Controlling a plane

To control the aircraft, the pilot moves the
control column from side to side to operate
the ailerons. Moving the control column
back or forward operates the elevators. The
foot pedals move the rudder from side to side.

FACT BOX

• Many flight terms are borrowed from terms
used on board ships, for example rudder,
port (left) and starboard (right).

• It takes an airliner one minute and nearly
2km/1 mile of airspace to reverse its course.

• A cruising airliner loses 3 tons in
weight every hour as fuel is used up.

• Many aircraft use computer-controlled
autopilot systems. These automatically set
the controls for take-off and landing.

• To control a helicopter, the angle of the
rotor blades is adjusted. This allows the pilot
to hover, go straight upwards, forwards,
backwards and even sideways.

MAKE A MODEL PLANE

THE previous two pages explained how the control surfaces on the wings and the tail of an aircraft work – they change the way air flows over the aircraft, allowing the pilot to steer the aircraft in different directions. Working together, the ailerons and rudder make the plane turn (bank) to the left or right. Moving the elevators on the tail makes the nose of the plane go up or down. This project shows you how to make a model plane, allowing you to see for yourself how the control surfaces work. Although a model is much smaller than a real full-size aircraft, it flies in exactly the same way. The scientific rules of flying are the same for any aircraft, from an airliner weighing 350 tons to this simple model made from pieces of paper, adhesive tape and a drinking straw.

You will need:
pencil, ruler, paper, scissors, glue,
adhesive tape, drinking straw, paper clip.

Make a model plane

1 Cut 2 rectangles, one 22 x 10cm/ 10 x 4in, the other 20 x 4cm/ 9 x 2in. Mark two ailerons 5cm/2½in long on the larger one, and elevators and the midline on the smaller one.

2 To make the wings, fold the larger rectangle over a pencil. Stick the top edge along the line you have drawn for the ailerons. Make cuts to allow the ailerons to move.

3 To make the tail, fold the smaller rectangle in half twice to make a W. Stick its middle together to make the upright fin. Make cuts to allow the rudder and elevators to move.

4 Use adhesive tape to stick the wings and tail to the straw (the plane's fuselage or body). Position the wings about three-quarters of the way along the fuselage.

5 Try adjusting the control surfaces. Bend the elevators on the tail slightly up. This will make the plane climb as it flies. Bend the elevators down to make it dive.

6 Bend the left-hand aileron up and the right-hand aileron down the same amount. Bend the rudder to the left. This will make the plane turn to the left as it flies.

7 Bend the right-hand aileron up and the left-hand aileron down. Bend the rudder slightly to the right and the plane will turn to the right. Can you make it fly in a circle?

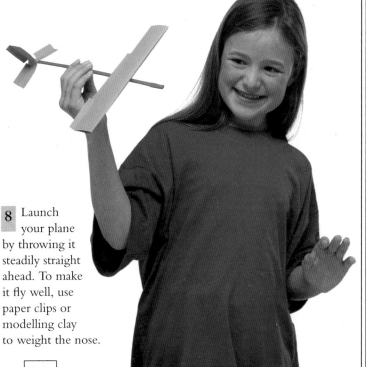

8 Launch your plane by throwing it steadily straight ahead. To make it fly well, use paper clips or modelling clay to weight the nose.

PROPELLERS

A LL aircraft need thrust to push them through the air. A propeller whirling at high speed converts the power of an aircraft's engine into thrust. Propellers have two or more blades, each shaped like a long thin aerofoil (airfoil) wing. The blades generate lift in a forward direction as they move through the air. Modern propellers have variable-pitch blades, which allow the pilot to alter the angle that the blades bite into the air. Changing the pitch of a propeller is like changing gears on a bicycle. For take-off, the front of the blades point forwards and the engine spins very fast to generate maximum thrust. Less thrust is needed when cruising. To cruise, the blades are set at a sharper angle and the engine spins more slowly. This arrangement gives the most economical use of fuel.

Propellers screw their way through the air, in the same way a screw goes into wood. For this reason, aircraft driven by propellers are often known as airscrews. As the propeller turns, the blades strike the air and push it backwards. This produces thrust and moves the aircraft forwards.

The DH.88 Comet
The de Havilland DH.88 Comet took part in a race from England to Australia in 1934. It is shown here after it was restored for the fiftieth anniversary of the race. Each of its propellers is driven by its own engine. They are like huge car engines and are fuelled by petrol.

Wooden propellers
The first aircraft had propellers made from layers of wood glued together. The pilot would spin the propeller by hand to start the engine – a potentially dangerous job if the pilot was hit.

Microlight

If you attach an engine-driven propeller to a hang glider, the result is a microlight. The engine in this microlight develops about the same power as a small family car. The twin-bladed propeller is less than 1m/3ft across. It pushes the plane along at around 65km per hour/36 miles per hour.

Lockheed Hercules

This aircraft carries military supplies. Each propeller has four variable-pitch blades. The propellers are driven by a turboprop engine, a type of jet engine.

Piper Seneca

The propellers on this four-seater plane each have two blades. They are twisted at an angle like the blades of a fan. As the propellers spin, the blades force air backwards.

MAKE A PROPELLER

MATERIALS

You will need:
ruler, pencil, thin paper,
scissors, paper clip.

A PROPELLER works in two different ways, each the opposite of the other. When a propeller spins, it makes air move past it. Propeller-driven aircraft use this effect to produce thrust. Also, when air moves past a propeller, it makes the propeller spin. These projects look at propellers working in these two different ways. In the first you can make a simple paper propeller called a spinner. As the spinner falls, moving air rushes past the blades, making it revolve. In the second project, you can make a spinning propeller fly upwards through the air. The propeller blades are set at an angle, like the blades of a fan. They whirl around and make air move. The moving air produces thrust and lifts the propeller upwards.

Children first flew propellers like this 600 years ago in China.

Make a spinner

1 Take a piece of paper, about 15 x 9cm/6 x 4in, and draw a T shape on it as shown in the picture above. With a pair of scissors, cut along the two long lines of the T.

2 Fold along the two short lines to make two wings and a stalk as shown above. Attach a paper clip to the bottom. Open the wings flat to make two blades. Now drop the spinner – what happens?

Before dropping it again, try giving each blade a twist to make your spinner spin round faster.

Make a propeller

1 With compasses, draw a circle 10cm/4in across on the cardboard. Draw a smaller circle 2cm/1in across in the middle. With the protractor, draw lines across the circle, dividing it into 16 equal sections.

2 Cut along the lines to the circle in the middle. Twist the blades up and down a little to angle them.

3 Make a hole in the middle of the cork slice with the bradawl. Put glue on the end of the dowel and push it into the hole. Stick the cork in the middle of the propeller.

MATERIALS

You will need: cardboard, ruler, pair of compasses, protractor, pen, scissors, 1cm/½in slice of cork, bradawl, dowel, model glue, cotton reel, string.

4 When the glue has dried, wind a long piece of string around the dowel. Drop the dowel into the cotton reel launcher. You are now ready for a test flight.

5 Pull steadily on the string to whirl the propeller around. As the end of the string comes away, the blades produce enough thrust to lift the spinning propeller out of the launcher and into the air.

JET ENGINES

Most large modern aircraft are driven by jet engines. Jet-propelled aircraft fly faster than propeller-driven ones. They can fly high where the air is thin and drag is less. Jet engines have huge fans inside that suck in air and compress it. Fuel burns in the air to produce a roaring jet of hot gases that blasts from the rear of the engine, producing thrust. Turbojet engines are fitted to some fighter aircraft. They are very powerful, but noisy, and use enormous amounts of fuel. Passenger jets use turbofan engines that have an extra-large fan at the front of the engine. This fan produces most of the thrust by forcing air around the engine so that it joins up with the jet of exhaust gases at the rear.

An octopus uses jet propulsion to move fast. It sucks in water and squeezes it out through a small hole. The jet of water pushes it along.

Compressor

Turbine

Cold air sucked in by fan

Exhaust gases

Combustion chamber

A turbofan engine
Jet engines are tube-shaped. Fast-spinning fans compress air into the jet engine. Fuel burns in the air and heats it. The exhaust gases spin the turbine that drives the compressor. Expanding gases leave the engine at over 2,000m per second/6,000ft per second. The blast of hot gases pushes the engine, and the aircraft, forwards.

Inside a jet engine
This jet engine is shown with its protective casing removed for inspection. You can see the huge blades at the front that suck in air. Most of the small pipes supply fuel and lubricating oil to the parts inside.

Executive jet
Small commuter jets carry people on trips. Its engines are on the tail, not on the wings, and can reach 790km per hour/480 miles per hour – nearly as fast as a large airliner.

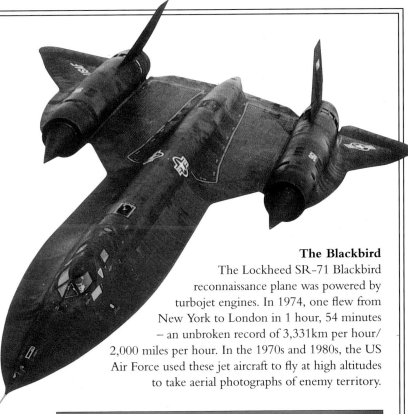

The Blackbird
The Lockheed SR–71 Blackbird reconnaissance plane was powered by turbojet engines. In 1974, one flew from New York to London in 1 hour, 54 minutes – an unbroken record of 3,331km per hour/ 2,000 miles per hour. In the 1970s and 1980s, the US Air Force used these jet aircraft to fly at high altitudes to take aerial photographs of enemy territory.

Jumbo jet
The Boeing 747 was the very first of the wide-bodied jets. Introduced in 1970, it has made international jet travel commonplace.

Helicopter
This helicopter is powered by a turboshaft engine, a type of jet engine without a jet of gases. Most of the energy turns the rotors. Only a tiny bit helps to push the helicopter forwards.

JETS AND TURBINES

T HE previous pages explained how a jet engine produces thrust from a roaring jet of super-hot gas. The jet engine looks complicated, but the way it works is very simple. A jet moving in one direction produces thrust in the other direction. Imagine you are standing on a skateboard and squirting a powerful hose forwards. Jet propulsion will push you backwards. This reaction has been known about for nearly 2,000 years, but it was not until the 1930s that it was used in an engine.

In the first project, you can make a jet zoom along a string. The jet engine is a balloon that produces thrust from escaping air. The second project shows you how a set of blades called a turbine works. It uses hot air to turn the blades. When trying out this project you must ask an adult to help you light the candles. These projects may seem very simple, but they use the same scientific principles that propel all jet aircraft through the air.

You will need:
long, thin balloon, drinking straw,
adhesive tape, scissors, string.

Make a balloon jet

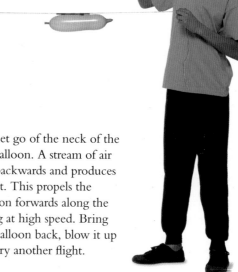

1 Blow up the balloon and, keeping a tight hold of the neck, tape the straw to its top. Thread the string through the straw. Stretch the string level across the room.

2 Let go of the neck of the balloon. A stream of air jets backwards and produces thrust. This propels the balloon forwards along the string at high speed. Bring the balloon back, blow it up and try another flight.

Make a turbine

1 Use a pair of kitchen scissors to cut out the bottom of a large foil pie dish.

2 Mark a smaller circle and 16 equal sections in the same way as on page 43 and cut along each one.

3 Angle the blades by twisting them slightly up and down. You have now made your turbine.

6 Make a hole in the middle of the turbine and place it over the pin. Ask an adult to light the candles. Hot air will spin the blades.

4 Tape the blunt end of the pin to one end of the dowel. Place the bead on the pin.

5 Put the dowel in the cotton reel and press the reel into modelling clay in the middle of the plate.

BREAKING THE SOUND BARRIER

THE sound barrier is like an invisible wall that travels in front of a speeding aircraft. Where does it come from? As an aircraft flies, it sends out pressure waves through the air. These waves are like the ripples around a moving boat. The waves move away from the aircraft at the speed of sound. When the aircraft is moving at the speed of sound the waves cannot outrun it. They build up and compress the air in front of the aircraft. To fly faster than the speed of sound, the aircraft must fly through this barrier of dense air and overtake it. The aircraft goes through the sound barrier with a jolt because drag increases suddenly. Shock waves spread out and can be heard on the ground as a rumbling sonic boom.

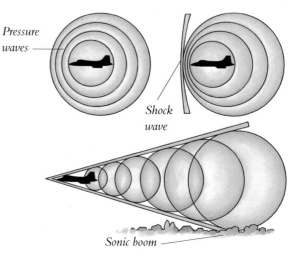

Pressure waves

Shock wave

Sonic boom

As an aircraft flies along, it sends out pressure waves. At the speed of sound, a shock wave builds up in front of the aircraft. As the aircraft accelerates through the sound barrier, the shock wave breaks away to be heard on the ground as a sonic boom.

Bell X-1 rocket plane
In 1947, the rocket-powered Bell X-1 was the first aircraft to travel faster than the speed of sound (which is called Mach 1).

The Bell X-1 was dropped from a B29 bomber at 6,000m/18,000ft. As it accelerated and climbed to 13,000m/39,000ft, the aircraft broke through the sound barrier.

Pilot's-eye view
A large transparent canopy gives the pilot a good field of view. Fighter pilots need an array of computers in the cockpit to cope with the enormous amounts of information they need to fly their jets.

Jet fighter

The Mirage flies at more than twice the speed of sound. It climbs almost straight upwards, speeding faster than a rifle bullet. It can reach the same height as a cruising airliner in about one minute. The Mirage is used by air forces around the world – different models can be used as fighters, fighter bombers and for reconnaissance.

Concorde
Concorde was the world's only supersonic passenger aircraft. It cruised at 2,175km per hour/1,300 miles per hour, over twice the speed of an ordinary airliner, and could cross the Atlantic Ocean in just over three hours. Its engines, however, were noisy and used a lot of fuel.

FACT BOX
• The speed of sound can change. It depends on air temperature and density. At sea level (20°C/68°F), Mach 1 is 1,225km per hour/ 735 miles per hour, but at 12,000m/36,000ft (-50°C/12°F) Mach 1 is 1,060km per hour/ 636 miles per hour.

• Subsonic speeds are below Mach 0.8 (jumbo jets). Transonic speeds are between Mach 0.8 and Mach 1.2 (breaking the sound barrier). Supersonic speeds are between Mach 1.2 and Mach 5 (Concorde and fighter jets). Hypersonic speeds are above Mach 5 (the Space Shuttle during re-entry).

• The first supersonic civilian aircraft to fly was the Russian Tupolev Tu-144 in 1968.

GOING UP

WATCH a bird taking off. It flaps its wings and up it goes! A modern airliner must hurtle down a runway as fast as a racing car. It has to travel 3km/2 miles to reach take-off speed, when its wings lift it off the ground. Some special types of aircraft are designed to take off and land on a single spot. These are called Vertical Take-Off and Landing aircraft (or VTOL for short). Examples include the famous Harrier jump jet and an early prototype, nicknamed the *Flying Bedstead* because of its very peculiar appearance. Helicopters, too, are VTOL aircraft, but the main disadvantage of helicopters is that they are slow compared to planes and use a lot of fuel. Other aircraft are designed to use very short runways a few hundred metres/yards long. They are called Short Take-Off and Landing aircraft (STOL). They can fly from inner-city airports or from remote airstrips in fields or deserts.

The Flying Bedstead *from the 1950s was built to experiment with ideas about vertical flight. Moving nozzles directed the thrust from a jet engine. Experiments with this machine helped to design the Harrier jump jet.*

Forward flight

Transition to forward flight

Take-off

Harrier jump jet
The engine of a jump jet has four nozzles fitted to its exhaust. At take-off, the nozzles deflect the jet exhaust down, so the plane goes straight up. When the nozzles swivel backwards the jet moves forwards.

De Havilland Dash 7
This aircraft is used on short runways
in cities. It has four extra-quiet engines
and can carry up to 54 passengers. Its large
wings provide plenty of lift and are set high on its
body to keep the propellers clear off the ground. The
Dash can take off on a runway just 700m/2,100ft long.

Autogyro

The autogyro is a cross between an plane
and a helicopter. The rotor is not driven by
the engine. During flight, rushing air spins
the rotor which provides most of the lift to
keep the autogyro up in the air.

Bell-Boeing Osprey

The Osprey is known as a tilt-rotor aircraft. The giant propellers
are called proprotors. Mounted at the tips of the wings, they tilt
upwards for take-off, like a helicopter. For forward flight, they
swing into the propeller position of a plane. The Osprey can fly
about three times as far as a helicopter on the same fuel load.

STRANGE AIRCRAFT

MANY aircraft have strange shapes. The Beluga looks like an enormous rotund dolphin with wings. The fabric used to make the wings of a pedal-powered aircraft is so thin, light shines through it. In all cases, an aircraft's strange appearance is due to its special design for a particular purpose. The Beluga is designed to carry large items that will not fit into the cargo hold of an ordinary transport plane. Pedal-powered aircraft must be ultralight so their wings are covered in thin plastic films. The people who design new planes are called aeronautical engineers. They can design planes for all sorts of different purposes – to carry enormous loads, to fly super-fast, or even to fly non-stop around the world. But no matter how strange an aircraft looks, it must be designed to take off, fly straight and level, and to land safely.

The Optica observation plane was designed for low-speed flight and to give a clear view. It is used to observe such things as problems with traffic flow or crop growth.

Pedal power

Gossamer Albatross was the first pedal-powered aircraft. A strong man has less power than a lawn mower engine, so the ultralight plane was made of thin plastic stretched on ribs 6mm/¼in thick.

World voyager

In 1986, *Voyager* took nine days to fly Americans Jeana Yeager and Dick Rutan non-stop around the world without refuelling. Each wing of the specially built plane was four times the length of the fuselage, providing the greatest lift with the lowest drag.

Invisible fighter

The F-117 Nighthawk stealth fighter is made up of flat, slab-shaped panels and special materials. These scatter beams from enemy radars and make the plane almost undetectable. Ordinary aircraft reflect radar beams straight back so they can be spotted. The F-117's low, flat shape reflects radar waves in directions other than back to the receiver, while special paint absorbs some of the radar waves.

A whale of a plane

The Airbus Beluga transport plane can carry up to 47 tons of cargo in its 7m/23ft-high hold. The Beluga is enormous, but it has the streamlined shape of a dolphin to help reduce drag.

Solar power

Solar Challenger was the world's first solar-powered aircraft. Weighing 59kg/125lb, it is still the lightest powered aircraft. Solar cells on the wings changed sunlight into electricity. An electric motor drove the propellers.

FACT BOX

• In 1907, one of the first British powered flights was made in a bizarre looking multiplane known as the *Venetian Blind*. It had nearly 50 sets of wings.

• The aircraft with the longest wingspan was a flying boat, the *Spruce Goose*. Designed by eccentric millionaire Howard Hughes, it had a wingspan of over 97m/300ft. It made its first and only flight in November 1947.

• Large, propeller-driven planes are used to scoop up huge amounts of water from lakes. They then drop their load like a water bomb to put out a forest fire.

FLYING THROUGH WATER

This boat is using hydrofoils to lift its hull completely clear of the water. At rest, it floats on the water like a normal boat.

Some boats have underwater wings, called hydrofoils. As the boat speeds along, the hydrofoils lift it upwards, out of the water. The hull of the boat is now moving in the air, so drag is greatly reduced. Hydrofoil boats can travel at 100km per hour/60 miles per hour, over three times as fast as an ordinary boat. Hovercraft seem to fly across the sea, very close to the surface of the water. Powerful fans blow air down through a rubber skirt to provide a cushion of air. This cushion cuts down the friction between the hovercraft and the water below. Propellers drive the hovercraft forward at up to 120km per hour/72 miles per hour.

MATERIALS

You will need: the lid of a margarine container, scissors, stapler, bradawl, pliers, coat hanger wire (ask an adult to cut out the bottom section).

How a hydrofoil works

1 Cut a rectangle of plastic, about 5 x 10cm/2 x 4in, from the lid of the container. Fold it in half to make a hydrofoil. Staple the ends together 1cm/½in in from the back edge.

2 Use a bradawl to make two holes in the front of the hydrofoil 1cm/½in away from the front edge. Use pliers to bend one end of the wire. Slide the hydrofoil on to the wire.

3 Try moving your hydrofoil in air – it will not lift up. Pull it through water and it will rise up the wire.

How a hovercraft works

1 Use a pencil to poke a hole through the middle of the polystyrene tray. The hole should be about 1cm/½in across.

2 Blow up the balloon with the pump and push its neck through the hole. Keep pinching the neck of the balloon to stop the air escaping.

3 Keep pinching with one hand, using the other hand to slip the button into the neck. The button will control how fast the air escapes.

You will need: polystyrene (Styrofoam) tray, pencil, balloon, balloon pump, button.

4 Place the tray on a table. Air escapes steadily from under the tray's edges, lifting it up fractionally. Give the tray a gentle push and it will skate along.

A hovercraft's rubber skirt is the black part just above the water. You can see how the air cushion makes the water spray about. Four large propellers drive the hovercraft in any direction.

ROCKETS AND SPACEFLIGHT

WHY can an aircraft not fly off into Space? The main reason is that there is no air in Space. Air becomes thinner higher up. Wings need air to provide lift, so planes cannot fly above about 40,000m/130,000ft. Jets use oxygen from the air to burn fuel. There is not enough oxygen for them to work properly above about 25,000m/65,000ft. Rockets can work in Space because they carry oxygen with them. There are two main types of rocket: liquid-fuelled rockets and solid-fuelled rockets. Liquid-fuelled rockets carry liquid oxygen to burn their fuel (liquid hydrogen). Solid-fuelled rockets are like enormous fireworks. They contain chemicals that release oxygen when heated.

Blast-off
The Space Shuttle had three liquid-fuel engines. They burned a mixture of liquid oxygen and liquid hydrogen from a strapped-on tank. Extra thrust came from two solid-fuel booster rockets. The tank and boosters fell away when their fuel was used up.

Landing Shuttle
The Space Shuttle took off like a rocket, but landed like a glider. It would glide down towards a runway just like an ordinary aircraft and deploy a parachute to help it roll to a stop. The Shuttle was used on a total of 135 missions between 1981 and 2011.

FACT BOX

• Liquid oxygen is stored at -183°C/-297.4°F; liquid hydrogen at -255°C/-427°F.

• The engines of the Space Shuttle would develop 2,200 tons of thrust at take-off – 20 times more than the engines of a jet airliner.

• To escape the Earth's gravity, a rocket must reach a speed of 11.2km per second/7 miles per second. This is called the escape velocity. If a rocket does not reach this speed, gravity will pull it back.

• Solid-fuel rockets were invented in China nearly 1,000 years ago. They were fuelled by gunpowder and were used to scare enemies.

Syncom

This communications satellite relays radio and TV signals all around the world. It was taken into Space by the Shuttle and it is held in orbit by the Earth's gravity. It is moving at a fast enough speed to prevent it from falling back to Earth.

Meteosat

This weather satellite was carried into Space by the Shuttle, which entered only a low Earth orbit. A small rocket pushed the satellite 35,000km/ 21,000 miles farther out. From this height it can send pictures of half the Earth's surface.

Ariane

A three-stage rocket, Ariane has three rockets mounted one above the other. After take-off, the first stage falls away when its fuel is used up. The second stage then fires, followed by the third.

Inside a rocket

Oxygen

Hydrogen

Combustion chamber

Liquid hydrogen and liquid oxygen are pumped into the combustion chamber. The hydrogen burns furiously in the oxygen. The exhaust produces immense thrust.

Probing into Space

This picture shows the Space probe *Galileo* approaching the planet Jupiter in 1995. Launched by the Shuttle, it used the gravity of the planets to accelerate it towards its destination.

MAKE A ROCKET

Rockets have powerful engines used to carry satellites into orbit 320km/200 miles or more above the Earth's surface.

SPACE rockets rely on jet propulsion to fly. A stream of hot gases roars out from the tail end and the rocket surges forward. Deep under the sea, octopuses rely on jet propulsion to escape from their enemies. They squirt out a jet of water and shoot off in the opposite direction. This project shows you how to make and fly a rocket that uses jet propulsion. The thrust of a rocket depends on the mass of propellant it shoots out every second. Water is a much better propellant than hot gas because it is so much heavier. Follow these instructions and your rocket could fly to more than 25m/75ft above the ground. You may need adult help to make some parts of this rocket and to launch it. When you are ready for a test flight, set your rocket up in an open space, well away from trees and buildings. This rocket is very powerful – you must not stand over it while it is being launched. Wear clothes that you do not mind getting very wet!

Make a rocket

MATERIALS

You will need:
card, pen, coloured card, scissors, plastic bottle, adhesive tape, funnel, jug (pitcher) of water, cork, bradawl, air valve, plastic tubing, bicycle pump.

1 Rockets have fins to make them fly straight. Draw out this fin template (it is about 20cm/8in long) on to plain card and use it to cut out four fins from coloured card.

2 Decorate your bottle to look like a rocket. Fold over the tab at the top of each fin. Use long pieces of strong adhesive tape to firmly attach the fins to the bottle.

3 Use the funnel to half-fill the bottle with water. (The water is the propellant. Compressed air above the water will provide the energy that makes the thrust.)

4 Use the bradawl to drill a hole through the cork. Push the wide end of the air valve into the plastic tubing. Push the valve through the hole in the cork.

5 Push the cork and valve into the neck of the bottle. Make sure it is pushed in firmly so that the cork does not come out too easily.

6 Attach the other end of the plastic tubing to the bicycle pump. Turn your rocket the right way up – you are now ready to launch your rocket outside. Look for a launch site well away from trees and buildings.

7 Stand the rocket on its tail fins. Start pumping. Bubbles of air will rise up through the water. When the pressure in the bottle gets high enough, the cork and water will be forced out and the rocket will fly upwards.

THE HISTORY OF FLIGHT

SINCE ancient times, human beings have wished they could fly. The first people to get off the ground were the Chinese – they used kites to lift people into the air over 700 years ago. In the 18th century, lighter-than-air balloons carried their first passengers and in 1852 the world's first airship flight occurred. But it was not until the invention of the petrol engine in the 1880s that true powered flight in a heavier-than-air machine became possible. In 1903, the Wright brothers made the world's first powered, controlled and sustained flight in their aircraft, *Flyer 1*.

About 500 years ago, the Italian artist and inventor Leonardo da Vinci drew many designs for flying machines. His scientific ideas about flight were correct, but a human could not provide enough power to make them work.

Clément Ader

In 1890, Ader's steam-driven aircraft *Eole* became the first full-sized plane to leave the ground. It managed to hop 50m/150ft. However, it was not considered true powered flight because it was uncontrolled.

Otto Lilienthal

German experimenter Otto Lilienthal built hang gliders in the 1890s from reeds covered with shirt material. He made over 2,000 flights and showed how curved aerofoil (airfoil) wings work better than flat ones. He was the first person to make repeated, controlled flights, but while making a test flight, Lilienthal crash-landed and died.

Orville and Wilbur Wright
On 17 December 1903, American inventor Orville Wright flew *Flyer 1* for 36m/108ft at a height of 3m/9ft. This was the first time a human had made a controlled powered take-off, flight and landing.

Louis Blériot
In 1909, Frenchman Louis Blériot became the first person to fly across the English Channel. At an average speed of 60km per hour/ 36 miles per hour, it took him 37 minutes. He said he had to wrestle with the controls to keep his monoplane flying steadily. The picture shows a modern replica of his plane.

Charles Lindberg
In 1927, American Charles Lindberg was the first person to fly alone and non-stop across the Atlantic Ocean in his tiny Ryan monoplane, *The Spirit of St Louis*. He took 33 hours and 39 minutes to fly 5,800km/3,600 miles from New York to Paris, flying at 173km per hour/120 miles per hour.

FACT BOX
- 1908 Orville Wright made the first sustained, powered flight lasting one hour.

- 1937 the jet engine was designed by British engineer Frank Whittle.

- 1939 American engineer Igor Sikorsky designed the first modern helicopter.

- 1947 the first aircraft flew at supersonic speed in the USA.

- 1952 the first jet airliner, the de Havilland DH 106 Comet, entered service in the UK.

- 1970 Boeing 747 jumbo jet entered service.

- 1976 Concorde started transatlantic service.

FLIGHT INTO THE FUTURE

BIRDS have been flying for more than 30 million years. Humans first took to the air 200 years ago. Now the air is full of aircraft of all descriptions. You can fly half-way around the world in under 24 hours. Some planes fly three times faster than sound. So what does the future hold? Look up into the sky in ten years' time and what will you see? Engineers are developing new and more powerful engines, new resin materials that are lighter and stronger than metal, and strange new wing shapes to help aircraft fly faster and higher. Whatever happens, human flight will increase – but at what cost to the health of our environment and the birds and animals who share it?

The Boeing 747-400 can carry up to 660 passengers. It is a double-decker version of the 1970s' jumbo jet. The newest version of the aircraft, the 747-8, is designed to be quieter, more economical and more environmentally friendly.

Horizontal Take-Off and Landing (HOTOL)
This picture is an artist's impression of HOTOL riding piggy-back to 15,000m/45,000ft on the Antonov An-225 (the world's largest plane). It then uses rocket engines to fly into Space. Moving at Mach 5, it could fly from the UK to Australia in under four hours.

FACT BOX

• A Russian experimental plane, called the Aquatain, has been designed to gain extra lift by skimming across the surface of the ocean. The craft is reported to use much less fuel than a conventional aircraft.

• All new planes have to meet strict environmental rules governing noise levels and emissions that might further damage the sensitive ozone layer.

• Modern cockpits use advanced systems to reduce the pilot's workload. Holographic displays and keyboards project data on to a see-through screen, while optical fibres carry signals at the speed of light to the aircraft's control surfaces.

Super Haas

Part of the Haas family of rocket launchers currently being developed, Super Haas is a ground-launched orbital two-stage piloted rocket. The first stage consists of seven Haas 2 rockets, while the second stage will be fitted with two Executor Plus rocket engines. Super Haas is intended to be the first Romanian rocket to launch a cosmonaut into orbit.

Supersonic Jets

The diagram shows (from top to bottom) turbojet, ramjet and scramjet engines. Ramjets and scramjets have three basic components: an inlet, where incoming air is compressed and decelerated; a combustor, where fuel is burned with atmospheric oxygen to create heat; and an outlet, where the heated air is accelerated to create thrust. Rather than use rotating parts, the speed of the aircraft itself compresses the air. Scramjet (supersonic combustion ramjet) engines do not decelerate the flow to subsonic speeds. An aircraft using this type of engine could greatly reduce travel times, potentially putting any place on Earth within a 90-minute flight. Scramjets could also allow cheaper access to Space.

Spaceplane

Skylon is a British design for an unpiloted, reusable spaceplane capable of reaching orbit in a single stage. During re-entry, the relatively light vehicle would fly back through the atmosphere and land on a runway. It could then fly again within two days. Testing of the key technologies was completed in November 2012.

INDEX